T0142437

SHATTERED,
NO LONGER
BROKEN

SHATTERED, NO LONGER BROKEN

SHANNON MARTIN

SHATTERED, NO LONGER BROKEN

iUniverse books may be ordered through
booksellers or by contacting:

iUniverse
1663 Liberty Drive
Bloomington, IN 47403
www.iuniverse.com
1-800-Authors (1-800-288-4677)

ISBN: 978-1-5320-8583-3 (sc)
ISBN: 978-1-5320-8584-0 (e)

Print information available on the last page.

iUniverse rev. date: 12/13/2019

ACKNOWLEDGEMENT

This book is dedicated to God, my Lord and Savior, for his Mercy, always guiding me and never leaving my side, no matter what I was going through. For giving me continued faith, strength through all the tears, and trials for continuing to fight to find myself, and for the courage and confidence to share my story in hopes of helping others.

For my Children, who are my strength, my hope, my legacy. Always, an "I love You", so much laughter, and love, never a dull moment.

For my precious Grandchildren who always put a smile on my face, and fill my heart with such joy and happiness.

Shannon Martin

For all my girlfriends that give me continued strength, courage and so much laughter everyday. For your inspiration, acceptance and encouragement to be who I am.

For all the Beautiful, strong, courageous Women that have been a part of my recovery. I could not have done this without your support, and your strength.

For my Father, thank you for being you, teaching me so much, even when you didn't realize what you were doing.

For my Sister, thank you for sharing this life with me.

For my past relationships, thank you for forcing me to become the Woman I am today, giving me the courage to learn who I am and who I want to be. With complete forgiveness, I hope you have true happiness.

This book is for all of you Mothers, women, Fathers, men, Sons, Daughters, and anyone else that has been struggling with life's problems, trying to control those problems of others as well as yourself, and learning how to truly take care of yourself during these times so that you do not become deeper and deeper in despair. I am sharing my story in hopes that it may help you all see that things very imperfect, can end with peace. never give up hope, keep fighting, keep learning, growing and changing yourself as needed.

When I first started my own recovery I remember sitting in my very first recovery meeting thinking that everyone around me was absolutely crazy, why were they laughing? Why were they joyful? Why were they talking about letting go and not worrying and deeply depressed about what was going on at home without them? How was I supposed to not have a GPS system tracker on men I was in relationships with, not worrying about where they were or where they were going and up to? What am I supposed to be doing about my family members, incarcerated, not knowing what is happening with them? That was over seven years ago. I learned that letting go, was exactly what I needed to do in order to take care of myself and get off this hamster wheel of doing the same thing over and over again and expecting different results. I was visiting the prison trying to cater to others, trying to fix, and meet their every need, as well as trying to convince others that they needed to grow and change. I remember being very stressed to assist others with putting money in their account, money on the phone, the long day visits, to and from the facilities, and always worried that they would not be taken care of. I was in relationships with men, that had cheated on me numerous times, always forgiving and trying to forget but not able to know how to act, how to be, or what to do without constantly checking their phone, and monitoring their every move. My life became consumed with their behaviors, and I became obsessed with trying to change them, so much that my life was no longer my own, I could not see anything except these behaviors and at some points ending my life so that I did not have to feel this any longer. I was willing to do everything in my power to show them I loved and cared about them no matter what that meant for me, what I was feeling or going through, they knew they could count on me to help them with whatever they needed, and that is who I became. I had heard and read about self care, but I did not know what it meant to take care of myself, to consider my feelings, my wants, my needs and desires. I thought I knew what I wanted, but that was all secondary as to what the others around me needed and wanted. I thought I was happy in my life as long as I could show others how much I loved them, taking care of them, and their needs first and foremost. If I tried to state what I needed, or wanted I was told I was selfish, that I did not care, that I did not know how to love, and that I did not have feelings or understand what they were going through. I now after many, many years of trying to control and change others behaviors, have learned that self-care is the most important and vital part of not only my recovery but the recovery of others. By doing self-care I am taking care of myself, knowing what my needs and wants are, and continuing to live life the way that I enjoy it, with my happiness with my peace of mind.There is no price tag on peace of mind, once you find it, there will never be anything more important or worth more, it is absolutely priceless.

Shannon Martin

The key to my peacefulness, as I have never understood before; is that I have to set boundaries for myself. These boundaries are based on what my needs and wants are, to keep me at my peace; to make me feel safe, comfortable, without allowing others to disrupt that. Before understanding what boundaries were, I used to allow anything and everything to happen around me. People would talk to me the way they wanted, often more screaming, yelling, demanding, do whatever they wanted in my home, come and go, bring over whoever they wanted and participate in whatever activities they wanted to in my home. I allowed this, sort of went along with anything and everything to avoid any conflict, any hurt feelings, or thoughts that I did not care or support them. It took me a very long time to learn the concept of boundaries, that I can say I do not want to do something, or be a part of what others are doing. I realize now, that it is ok for others to do what they are wanting and going to do, but they can not do it around me, in my home, in my space. I learned that I can say no, that it is absolutely ok and necessary to set boundaries, and let others know what they are and that they will not be compromised for any situation or person. I learned that I can accept others and allow others to be who they are, to behave the way that they want to, and do what they choose to do, knowing that I have no control over any other person or situation. I learned the only person I have control over is myself, my actions, my boundaries, what I choose to tolerate, and how I choose to be treated.

When I first started my recovery program, I remember being asked what my boundaries were? I remember thinking about that for quite a while, then, it came to me that I did not know what boundaries were, and then when I learned, I realized that I had none. This stemming from my childhood, me learning as a young girl, not only not what boundaries were, but that there were none allowed by me, or others around me.

When I was growing up, I had very little stability with my Mother, I had no idea who was coming, where we were going, or what was going to happen next. I did not know who was going to show up for our visits, what kind of mood my Mother was going to be in that day. In Father's home, I had no privacy, my things would always be gone through, my feelings were not allowed to be shared, I was told what I was going and needed to do, and that I was always going to be like my Mother. I felt like I was non existent, I felt like I lived in a world where I was always questioning my reality, where I would wonder, "is this really happening". I learned at a very young age, not to think, or feel, I wondered if I was real, if others could see me, and often remember wondering if I was whispering when I was talking as nobody seemed to hear me. There was a very loud and clear message that seemed to come from all those around me, that was, that I should be thankful to be here, that I was saved, rescued, that I did not belong, but would be tolerated and reluctantly and resentfully given what I needed. I remember so vividly not expecting anything, not voicing anything, not feeling anything, but going along and always doing what others wanted and expected of me.

This continues to be who I am from a very young age through my later adult years. When I was in grade school, I remember, I would let boys touch me in ways I knew that that I did not want, but was not able to say anything. I remember specifically allowing boys at the pool we went to in the summertime, to pull down my top, and then would laugh with them about it. My relationships in grade school, and high school continued to be the same way. I never felt good enough, feeling thankful and lucky if someone talked to me or even noticed me. My first serious relationship in high school; I remember when he first spoke to me, I turned and looked to see who he was really talking to, and I asked him if he was talking to me? I couldn't believe it, I was so excited that he was talking to me, that he picked me, so excited and in disbelief, that I allowed him to be physically, sexually, and emotionally abusive to me, again always putting his needs first, only seeing his needs, wants, and ignoring any that I may have had, did I even have any? I think I was just thankful that someone heard me, saw me, noticed me. I left him eventually, but only after starting a new relationship with a much older man, who beat him up for abusing me. I felt so treasured, so alive, after that, thinking that he protected me, stood up for me, and seemed to love me, and understand me.

I fell for him instantly, finally, someone to rescue me from all this numbness I have been feeling. He ended up being the same way, very broken from his own past abuse. Using drugs, alcohol, and having multiple affairs. I eventually started the cycle all over again, begging him to stop drinking, using, seeing other women. I remember hiding his keys, trying hard to control his behaviors, and convince him to change. I would again be the one, begging him to stay after his cheating, trying to convince him that I mattered. He was also very abusive, I remember so vividly the fights, the abuse, I allowed him to beat on me to relieve his stress or whatever he was going through, I never even thought about myself and what all that abuse was doing to me, and I looked forward to all the gifts, and the make up period, where he would really seem to love and care about me, really seemed to know me, hear me, and want to be with me. The night I finally got enough courage to stand up to him was when we were having a fight on Halloween night, over not letting my young children, go trick or treating, I had a bad migraine and had asked him to go with us to help out, he eventually had me against the wall, yelling and punching me and my oldest Son came up and kicked him, and was hitting him, he then picked up my Son and threw him across the room, it was then, because of what he did to my Son, that I realized there was a problem, and started finding the courage to change things. Again, not considering my feelings, wants or needs, but my young Sons. While I did seem to have courage to start looking at my life, and change some things, these thoughts of not being good enough, being deserving enough would continue. I remember how I continued to look for the same type of men, someone, I could "help". Someone that needed me, someone that could see me. I soon became that woman that needed a mans approval, a man to tell her how valuable she was, someone to love and accept me, I then became dependent on my relationships with men for my own self worth, everything that I was doing was about that attention I got from my relationships. My weight, my physical appearance, I thought I was happy, raising my Children, and being a great Mother to them, and also in good relationships. Those relationships continued to be me not getting my needs met, but getting the attention I was getting was better than none, so

I desperately kept seeking men's approval and again thought that they loved me, understood me and would actually stick around for a while, which never in my life had happened.

I understand now., how desperate I was for that approval, for that feeling of belonging, being wanted, being valued, for my feelings to matter to someone, for me to be able to express those, and to have a voice, that I had always thought didn't matter, that I didn't matter. I allowed those people in my life who told me those things to control me and I would submissively feel that way for many, many years of my life. I was unaware of who I was, and what I wanted. I always tried to conform to be who others wanted and thought I should be. I had a vague idea of what I wanted in life, who I wanted to be, but that did not matter, as I tried to be what others needed and wanted from me.

I have learned that even though I am a very independent woman, that I am Co Dependent. I have learned to be dependent on others, dependent on their thoughts of me, dependent on what they think about where my life should go, what to do with my life, and not being able to function or follow my goals and dreams, because of my life becoming so consumed with others addictions, and behaviors. I have come to realize that even with all my accomplishments, for all the things that I should be happy and grateful for, that none of that matters as long as I am trying to control others lives and behaviors. I have realized in the midst of being suicidal, with a dramatic plan to take pills on my boyfriend's bed so he can find me, constant feelings of wanting to give up, wondering why I am still living? Wondering why I am here, what is my purpose and how I am going to continue my life without others and the past relationships I have been in? How am I going to move forward when I keep hearing those voices from my past, of being not good enough, not deserving, not worthy to be heard?

I have finally learned and have to constantly remind myself everyday, that focusing on others addictions and behaviors, keep me from looking at my own deficiencies, keep me stuck, and not able to make changes in my life that are needed. This keeps me doing the same things in relationships that I have always done, putting others needs before my own, then wondering why I keep having the same results, broken relationships, and dreams. I have learned that in order to make things better, the only thing you can change is yourself, that change is hard, we always want to go back to what is familiar, and comfortable, however, the only way to make things better is be uncomfortable, do what you are not used to doing, and most importantly be consistent. I was never consistent in my life, I would get mad and say things, make empty threats and promises, but then never followed through with anything, because I was afraid, worried that others would leave, worried about conflict, and upsetting others. People around me knew I never did what I said, I never made changes that I said and promised that I would, and things kept being the same. Over and over again, just like that hamster on the wheel from earlier. I struggled so hard to find answers as to how I could change this life that I have created, how I could change others around me to make them love me, respect me, what could I do to make them do those things I needed? The more I tried to be that person they needed, the more unhappy I became, and they were never happy, no matter what I did. I realized that I could no longer blame the men in my life, for being mean, manipulative, and cheating; that is who they were. I could no longer blame my children for making me feel sorry for them and manipulating me, due to their addictions. I could no longer blame my past, my childhood, my parents, all those people in my past who made me feel like I didn't matter, as they were not changing, unless they wanted to on their own, and it was not my duty, or responsibility to tell them they needed to change, or try to change them.

I realized what I have always heard, that the only people we can change is ourselves, I realized that no matter how long it took me or how difficult this journey was going to be for me that I could no longer continue to live this way. That is when I decided to finally get my own recovery, to look at myself for my behaviors, for changes that I needed to make, to once and for all understand, why I was the way I am, why my relationships are what they are, and what I can do to change myself. I had to change how I felt, why I thought this way, why I thought it was ok for others to treat me certain ways, why I did not feel empowered to respect myself enough to stop this pain I felt, and this overwhelming desire to take care of everyone and everything around me. I had dig deep into myself. I had to do some very difficult and painful soul searching to see where this was coming from, and what I could do to stop doing the same things over and over again, these behaviors of enabling others, not having any boundaries, or self respect for myself. After much research, I realized I did not want to look at, my own stuff, that is what kept me focused on everyone else, I realized that I was taught at a very young age, that I did not have a voice, that I did not matter, and that my job in life was to help others and make them feel better, regardless of how I felt. I realized that I became the caretaker for others early in my life, even though I was a child. I realized that I took on others hurt, pain, and behaviors. That their lives, became mine, if they were sick from their addictions, I took care of them, if they were sad, I tried to make them laugh, and feel better, regardless of what I was feeling. I learned that if they said mean things that hurt me, that I accepted that, and would quickly forgive them and try to forget what was said and done to me. I would push any physical or emotional pain away, so that I did not feel it, I stuffed my own pain, feelings, emotions deep inside and never showed anyone how I was feeling.

This led to a life of confusion, not feeling as if I mattered, that my feelings, thoughts, and my voice or anything I said mattered, that I was not enough, and that my purpose was to take care of others. I learned to stuff my feelings, and take care of others so that they would not be upset with me, want to leave me, or not have me around.

My first memories of this are not until I was about 5 or 6. I remember and can see just like yesterday, me making scrambled eggs for my little sister, in our small kitchen. I am not sure if my Mother was home, sleeping, or out, all I know is that we were hungry and I was used to taking care of my little sister, seeing her little eyes looking up at me. I used to take care of my Mother at this age as well, I remember specifically, worrying about her, helping her when she was sick from drinking and trying to make her get up from bed when she stayed out too late. I remember trying to be a good girl, trying to make her happy, trying to make her love me as I loved her, and how I used to beg her to change, to stay home, to not drink. How I wanted so bad for her love me and want to stay home and be with us, I used to crave her attention, for her to be the Mother other Kindergarten age girls had. I remember looking at my little blue eyed sister wondering what we had done, why were we not lovable, trying to comfort her, and then thinking of new ways I could get Mom to change, hide her keys, her alcohol, pretend to be sick, but none of that mattered at that time. I remember specifically writing her a note one day asking her to stay home, and telling her that I worried about her and that she was going to die and go to hell. I remember because she was very upset, and angry that I thought that way, I don't even remember how I learned about hell, it was not for about a year or so later that I would be going to church. My sister and I, at that time lived in an apartment with my Mother in California. I don't recall what city. One day after my sister and I went to school, I was in Kindergarten at that time. I remember specifically that day the disruption, yelling outside the classroom, people saying things outside the door, frantically yelling "you can't go in there, you can't be here". I had no idea what was happening, but then a man came into my classroom, and grabbed me up in his arms, ran with me down the hall, and put me in his car. I did not know this man, I did not know what was happening. My sister was also in the car, she was on the floor of the car looking scared and crying, I remember how happy I was even in this chaos that she was with me. I remember trying to hold her hand and comfort her, telling her everything was going to be ok. We drove in that car for several hours, there were other people in the car with us, people I did not know, people that I don't remember ever meeting before. There was 4 adults and my sister and I. We continued to cry, they tried to calm us down, explaining that the man was my Father. We cried for hours and were forced to sing 100 bottles of Pepsi on the wall, I hate that song to this day!. That was the day that my life as I knew it, changed forever. My Father had taken us from California, where we were living with my Mother, and they brought us back to Phoenix. My Dad introduced us to our new family.

It seemed like a long time after that day that I would see my Mother again. My stomach used to hurt so much, during that time, I was so worried about her, What would happen to her? Who would take care of her? How was she going to get through this, and was she even aware of what was happening and that we were gone? I remember my Father talking about my Mother, of course which were not nice, but I don't think I totally understood all of what was going on until the day that I had to go to court and sit in the front of all those people. I was in the middle of a custody battle, they were asking me who I wanted to live with? I had been with my Father for a short time now, and I liked him, but there were many more rules that I was not used to. I saw my Mother in the courtroom, sad, tearful, but also with that strong, angry, nobody getting to me look. I was so confused, my stomach hurt so bad, how do I answer these attorneys questions, why are they saying such mean terrible things about us, about my Mother? I remember the courtroom, the smell, the big chair I had to sit in, the questions, the stares from all the people, my Mother's face. Then the big question came; they asked me (remember I am maybe 6 at this time). Who do I want to live with? How do I answer this? How do I say I want to live with my Mother, and hurt my Father the one who just risked everything to get me? How do I say my Father and hurt my Mother even more than she is hurting now? I remember sitting on the stand in court, saying "I don't know; shrugging my shoulders, and looking at my parents, hurting so bad inside. My Dad was fighting for custody of us from my Mother. Saying all these horrible things, how we lived, how we were abused, abandoned, neglected. What did these things mean? I thought we were fine, I was taking care of my sister and I, we were good. My Mother saying things about my Father. All these thoughts, all these hurt feelings, all this pain in my stomach, the pain of my parents and Sister hurting so much, all these emotions that I kept inside, afraid to talk, to tell my thoughts and feelings out loud. I kept everything in, and prayed that there would be a solution for all this figured out soon.

My Father ended up getting custody of my sister and I. We stayed in Phoenix and lived as a big blended family, I remember pictures of all of us in family pictures, when we were newly introduced to the family, there were many half smiles, and really messed up haircuts. I was not allowed to see my Mother or have contact with her, only on the weekends, and as supervised by my Father and Stepmother. All those feelings that I had again, pushed aside. My feelings of not being able to share how I was feeling, I wanted to be with my Mother so badly, I wanted to run to her, and let her know that everything was going to be ok. I remember being told that I would have no contact with my Mother, I was explained the rules, and my Father told me that my Step Mom is now my Mother and made me call her Mom. I remember thinking, I did not want to do that, whenever I addressed her, I tried to not use a name at all, I remember trying to tell my Father how I was feeling, that I did not want to call her my Mother, how I did not feel comfortable, however, that did not matter, I was forced to call her Mom, and was apparently supposed to forget about my real Mother and past life. That is one of the first times I learned that my feelings were not important, and how no matter how I was feeling, I had to pretend that things were fine, and not to feel, because it did not matter anyway. I stuffed all my feelings inside, did what I was supposed to do, as I would continue to do for many years to come.

We went to school, went to church, and appeared as one big happy blended family. My Mother ended up getting visitation with my sister and I. She was able to pick us up on Saturdays for the day, eventually that would turn in to some over nights on the weekends. I remember the pain so vividly, the pain of my Father and Mother. I remember comments from others, "I am going to be just like my Mother, my Mother is no good, I should be thankful that they took us from my Mother, and more specifically how my Mother was a drunk, prostitute, and not fit. My Father asked me when I was a teenager once, why I wanted to cruise Van Buren, asking "do you think you may see someone you know", it took me many years to figure that out. The many jokes, the negative comments, not accepting me for who I was but always comparing me, to my Mother. Again, a constant reminder, that I did not matter, who I was did not matter, but already judged to be something created by others.

Today, I realize that others make comments and judgements about things that they really do not understand, based on being afraid to learn about others, accept others, and from things they are told by others. Many of these things have affected my self esteem, taught me what to expect from others, and have allowed me to feel negatively about myself for many, many years. I now realize that that is others fear, and changes in themselves they need to work on, and has absolutely nothing to do with me. I have learned and teach to others, that no matter our history, backgrounds, or where we came from we still can be anything we want to be.

I remember growing up we would visit my Mother, come home with new toys, and we would have to put them up, not allowed to express our happiness or joy from the gifts but put them away so that others feelings were not hurt. I used to wonder, where do we fit in. I remember not being included in many things, being intentionally left out of family activities. I remember feeling so sad, heart broken, feeling that I was not a part of any family, and not knowing where I truly fit in. I will continue to feel this way for most of my life. The pain and hurt of not fitting in, how I wanted to fit in, to be someone who mattered and belonged. I remember my Sister, my biological sister, appeared to be even more lost, I remember her shyness, her sad face, I used to feel so sorry for her, and tried to make her feel better. We tried to keep our close relationship, we would walk to school together, talk just the two of us. It became apparent that we were waiting for each other, and we eventually had new rules were we could not be in the room together by ourselves, and we would not be allowed to walk to school together, even though we were going to the same place. I would have to leave 20 minutes earlier than her, so that we didn't have that time to be together, I remember that when we were caught waiting for each other, and we would get in trouble, determined to not have us be close or talking with each other before school. Funny how when people try to make you not be close, the closer you really get. My Sister and I are very close to this day, and share a very special bond, that nobody will be able to tear apart.

I loved my sister so much, we remained close and understood each other like nobody else could understand us. She was so quiet, never spoke, just stared, she eventually developed a blinking disorder, where she would constantly blink her eyes, I remember her having to sit at the table forever, trying not to blink and getting in trouble for blinking her eyes. I remember all the punishments, cleaning the house constantly, babysitting, cooking dinners, the whippings with the belt, and as we got older, being grounded constantly as a way for punishment and control. My time with my Father was very limited, I was not allowed to go to him with my feelings, or my needs, if I expressed anything negative about the way things were, or what I thought, I would be punished. I realize now that all my emotions, not being allowed to feel what I was feeling, not being allowed to express my feelings, not feeling anything, feeling numb, stuffing my feelings inside, is how I learned to be Co-Dependent, and not have my own self worth or purpose. This is how I learned and will practice for many years to come that I did not matter, my feelings did not matter, that I was to keep quiet in my pain. I learned that I did not have a voice, and that I was powerless over what was going on with me. I hid my feelings, my emotions, realizing that only the needs of others were important. I learned that I needed to keep quiet, do what others told me to do and feel the way they told me to feel. I learned to avoid conflict at all times, not to speak up, but to keep these feelings inside of me. This is something I will continue to do throughout my life. Keeping my emotions and feelings inside, not expressing myself, being scared to say how I really felt, which continually set me up for failure in my future relationships. I learned that only other people's feelings mattered, and I would continue to do everything I could to make others happy, and try to make them love me.

I remember thinking how sad I was in my new situation, away from my Mother, living with strangers, but more than me, I remember thinking how sad my Father was. He seemed to look sad, overwhelmed, tired, mad, and angry. I saw he was trying hard, but he did not appear to be happy, we were not happy. I used to look at him and think about how I wish he was happy, I remember going to the wishing well at the mall and throwing pennies in there wishing that he and my Mother would get back together, so that he would be happy. Many years of my childhood and teenage years I would have angry, rebellious feelings stemming from my anger at my situation and being separated from my Mother.

My middle school days and teen age years were very interesting to say the least. Living with my Father who was never home, as he worked all the time, to make ends meet. He was such a hard worker, still is to this day. Visits continued with my Mother when she showed up. My sister and I would be ready and very happy to go on visits with her. My Mother and My Grandmother would show up, take us to lunch we would spend the day with my Grandmother, and her which were truly some of my happiest memories. My Mother would also on some days come by herself, well, she would come to our house by herself, always in a different car. My Mother had many boyfriends, I laugh as I am writing this, because she would pick us up in a Cadillac, we would wonder at first where it came from, but then got used to picking up her boyfriends who owned the car on the corner. This became usual, in between the many visits where she did not show, calling to say she wasn't coming, many, many times not calling or showing up. I remember how my sister and I would get up, get dressed and ready, and then she wouldn't show up. I remember more than once, my Grandmother picking us up, with my Mother being beat up, assaulted the night before in a bar fight, in jail, or too sick from drinking to pick us up. Again, more wishing that she would stop her behaviors, and love us enough to pick us up and spend time with us, I don't believe I ever blamed her or was angry at her, at these times, but felt sad, sad that we were not enough to make her change.

Let me tell you a little bit about My Mother. My Mother had me at age 15. She was one of 6 children. She was also part of a blended family, part from my grandmother and then part from her new marriage. Her step Father was sexually and physically abusive, it was not until after I was in my 40s and planning my Mothers funeral that I learned more about her, and how she was like me pretending to be so strong, and knowing that she really didn't matter or have a voice. My Aunt telling me that her step Father would sexually abuse all the older girls, and that often my Mother would often take the abuse so that her sister's did not have to take it. I should have realized earlier that my Mother was sexually abused, as I remember how worried she was, that it was going to happen to my sister or I. She would not allow us to be close to my Grandmother's Husband, she would not allow us to even talk to him. Protecting us from him as she did with her sisters. She soon became a victim of something so horrible that her life would be changed forever, these things and this abuse she would never be able to overcome or recover from. I remember when I was living with her in California that while she was gone, that one of her boyfriends made me put his penis in my mouth, It is haunting, remembering this now, the smell, the taste, the fear, that just never goes away. My Mother happened to come home home right in time and caught him, I was so scared, and was so thankful she walked in to save me. My Mother was so upset, so angry, she physically assaulted him, and I remember that she packed us up and left him. I didn't realize then, but do now, how she really tried to protect us, even though she was so young, and appeared to be so lost in her own way. My Mother was an alcoholic, and addict. She had many problems that came from her childhood that she was not able, regardless of how many times she tried, to overcome. My Mother passed away when she was 51 years old from Liver disease. That was one of the saddest days of my life, however, I am thankful for the years prior to her death, while in her sickness, I got to get to truly know my Mother, that vulnerable 14 year old girl, that she always tried hard not to be. I learned that she was not able to parent me appropriately due to her alcoholism and addiction, I learned that she was a very hurt, young girl, full of pain, pain that she did not know how to deal with, pain that was so severe that she turned to her addiction to mask it, she also turned to men and other people to feel her worth. It was in those years before my Mother's passing that I truly got to know and understand her. It was then that I was able to stop being so bothered by her. In her sickness I was able to see her heart, her soul, her struggles, her love for me, that I had thought for so long was non existent. Getting to know her, how much pain she endured, and seeing what she had overcome, I realized how much I truly loved her. She was one of the toughest women I have known, a fighter, not afraid of much, but yet, still deep inside that very frightened little girl. I love and miss her so much and can not wait to see her again in Heaven.

It was from those early moments in my life that I began to become confused as to who I was, where I fit in, and who I wanted to be. Moments where I felt the need to take care of everyone else, taking on my Mother's pain of her childhood, abuse, my Father's unhappiness, my sisters shyness, unhappiness, that I started learning that I needed to be all for everyone else. I learned that my feelings didn't matter, I learned that I should not even share my feelings, I learned that I was to be seen but not heard. I learned then that I had to be the peacemaker, then one that fixed everything, that one that had a plan to make everything better. I held my feelings in, never expressed myself, and became a woman from that point on that would look strong on the outside, but allow everyone else's feelings, emotions, behaviors, over ride her own, which eventually led me to a life of physical, and emotional abuse; becoming co-dependent on others and trying to control their addictions and behaviors.

I learned at a young age that I was expected to take care of others. I would come to realize that through all my experiences as a child, that what I deeply wanted and needed was to be loved by others, and feel that I belonged, with them, around them, and would do whatever it took to get that love and attention, even if they were abusive, or disrespectful, I was looking for anyone, which mostly meant the ones who needed help themselves, and knew that I would be willing to help them no matter what. I specifically remember in grade school having a nice boyfriend, we would hold hands under the pillow at my house. There were 4 girls in my blended family, so as a way of controlling us and keeping us from getting pregnant was to have my younger siblings in the room as a chaperone. I realized then, that I liked him, but I was craving something, something I didn't quite understand at the time, but felt like I was missing something. I was pretty popular in grade school, I was told I had "everything in the right place", and I was proud of that, even though now, I understand what that means and should not have been. As a young teen, I was always thinking I was fat, and was always on some trendy diet or work out plan to control me weight. There is a picture I remember of myself as a young girl, where I was lifting bricks on the picnic table, as I could not afford weights, and always thought it was important to keep up my physical appearance. Although thinking now, as much as I enjoyed working out, it was not for me, but for the attention I would get from others, and I think deep down I was looking for a way to feel better on the outside so I did not have to figure out what I was craving and missing, and was a way for me to feel better hiding and holding in the feelings I had inside me. From there as I remember the little girl I was, so lost, so needing to be loved and needing to fit in, I moved on to a world of chaos, relationships that would leave me void, hurt, confused, and feeling less than. I remember specifically going to high school, no longer popular, but feeling alone, afraid, and trying even harder to fit in somewhere. I remember hanging out with groups that I felt I would fit into. I did not know who I was, so tried to find others that liked me, that accepted me. I remember trying so hard, to find a group to fit in. I wanted so badly to try out for the softball team, I had been good as a younger child, and was told that because I was grounded for not cleaning properly that I could not try out for the team. I truly think that decision, caused me further and further to be lost, as one thing I really wanted, and could truly relate to, I was told I could not do.

When I started dating in High School, well I was not technically allowed to date, but my guy friends would come over and we would sit on the couch with the chaperone, and we would talk. The one I felt was so special, seemed to be everything I needed to make me feel loved. He seemed older, more mature, so handsome, and he drove already. My Father hated him, he would come over and they would tell him he couldn't wear shorts, or his baseball hat in the house. I was grounded constantly from seeing him, which led to me sneaking out, ditching school, and doing whatever I could do to be with him and see him. I remember being at his house, and there would be a knock on the door, being my Father, I would hide, get grounded, but the chaos continued. I lost my virginity to him at age 15 and I did everything I could do to prove to him that I love him, under no circumstances could he change that. It didn't take too long after our relationship started that I found out he was being with other girls. It was easy for him, I was always grounded, and only around when I could sneak off. I would listen to others tell me about what he was doing, who he was seeing, I wouldn't believe them of course, but sometimes I would confront him. When I did, the fights started, the physical abuse, so much anger, and violence. He used to hit me so hard, black eyes, bruises, all the heart aches. This went on for several years, always forgiving, accepting of being mistreated,because that is what I thought I deserved, and wanted to be looved. I started working early at age 15 ½ to get out of my house as well as earn my own money. I was working for $2.75 an hour, 2 jobs and going to high school. I was completely responsible for taking care of myself and well as supplying all his emotional, financial needs and doing anything he asked me to do regardless of the cost or consequences. I was hurt when he was hurt, I was hurt that I could not make him happy, I was hurt that he could not keep a job, I was hurt that he was abused as a child, and was adopted, I was hurt that he was so hurt that he had to beat me up to show me his pain. I took it all, I was completely responsible for him, as well as myself. I gave up myself, my friendships, my family, because continuing to date him with all my bruises, only made my Dad hate him more, and made me isolate from others around me. This was my first attempt to fix, change, and control others in my romantic relationships. I remember every time he cheated on me, and we fought, physically and emotionally, the pain I felt, then he said he would never do it again. I had so much hope, only to have it happen again and again. The last time I remember him cheating was when I had just gotten him another job at where I was working, a retail store. He could not keep a job, and was working sporadically, but kept getting fired for stealing money. I continued to keep risking everything and every part of myself for him, as I was so determined to make him happy. We were working at the retail store, I was smart, always a hard worker and working my way up, which seemed to come easy to me, considering my other side of being completely dependent on him. I remember one night after work that one of my co-workers told me that he was with another girl. I didn't believe it at first, but then found out from her, that she was seeing him, and may be pregnant from him. I couldn't believe this, why would this man do this to me after all I have done for him? I of course confronted him, and the violence started, this time a black eye, more bruises. I went to see my sister that evening, who had moved out of the house at 15 to live with my Aunt and Uncle and she told me that I needed to get away from him, that I needed to meet a new guy that she knew. I met him later that evening, and although I can honestly say that I was not attracted to him, and it was not love at first sight, as I remember, I was interested in him because he had his own place, and he was flashy, seemed to have that mean side to him, was older and was going to finally give me what I needed, to be loved and respected. I remember that he looked at my black eye, I told him about my boyfriend, and he went and beat him up, I understood that to be, him proving to me he how much he already loved me. He gave me what I desperately needed and wanted, showed me that I mattered enough to beat someone up for. He never allowed me to go back to him rescuing me from that relationship, and showed me how much he already liked me and was willing to do to show me that I mattered.

I started a new relationship with this man that rescued me from my past and all the abuse. I was so intrigued, infatuated to say the least. Shortly after I discovered that the life of abuse, and how I knew it before, would continue to be how it was. The names of the men changed, however, the pattern of abuse, care taking would continue for me, now bringing children into the equation. Some of the chaos was different, there was one late night when I remember waking up, and saw him and his friend shooting up Cocaine. I had never seen a needle in someone's arm, even though my Mother had probably used that way, many times, that is not something I had been familiar with. It was very scary, to say the least, and that vision will stay with me forever. However, this relationship will continue despite all the red flags and problems. The more behaviors he did that I did not agree with, the more I tried to control them, his drug use, drinking, and cheating. From that time on, our relationship continued to be very chaotic to say the least, many fights, verbally and physically, well I should say many one sided fights, as he yelled, told me what I wasn't doing right, and then would physically abuse me until I eventually apologized and everything was ok again, as long as I stayed quiet, didn't ask questions about what he was doing or where he was all night, or the days prior. There was a typical pattern of abuse, fights, hitting, yelling, screaming, him leaving coming back with gifts and sometimes apologies, this went on for many years, ups and downs, other women, affairs, gambling and as I found out later many illegal activities as well. I had no self esteem, no self worth, the only happiness I could find was through my children. I never had the strength to leave, this relationship, I had tried many times, once packing up my car only to be followed by him and threatened. I came back home and remember unpacking my car by myself as he was yelling and hitting me in between trips from the car. One night I remember very clearly I had gone out with my friends and he came and found me, he drove me home slamming my head into the window, and at one point we got out of the car close to our home at an irrigated church, and he held me under the irrigation water telling me he was going to kill me, he almost did. I remember when we got home, so embarrassed and ashamed, the babysitter looking at me all wet, like I was crazy. There was another time where he held a gun to my head because we were fighting about his drugs, and I would not smoke cocaine with him, so he put a loaded gun to my head, and shot it, thankfully, and by God's grace, it miraculously missed me, to this day, I have no idea how, other than God, how I was even alive. The gun was pressed against my head, there was no way physically possible, that it ended the way it did. There was a bullet hole in the closet from that day, that often reminded me to be grateful, and how God saved me, but even that was not enough to end this co dependent relationship. The reason that I finally got enough courage to leave this relationship is because we were fighting about me wanting him to go trick or treating, which apparently he other plans and was wanting to go out. As we were fighting, my oldest Son came and kicked him to get him to stop hitting me, he picked him up and threw him across the room, it was then, that it finally dawned on me that this man who I thought I loved so much, was never going to change, even though I had become so addicted to him the fights and chaos, not knowing anything different, that I finally had the courage to make him leave, I called the police, made him leave, and with every bit of courage in me, stuck to my decision. He disappeared for a while, I was raising my 3 children on own and doing well. I was working, and going to school to better myself, eventually getting my Bachelors degree in Social Work. I was able to go to school, knowing that I needed to be able to take care of myself, and my children, I think that is where I found much of my self fulfillment and self confidence to finally let go of my marriage and the abuse that came with it. Soon after getting my Bachelors degree, I was working 2 jobs trying to keep things together. I had recently watched my car be repossessed, and my furniture, boat, and other cars from my marriage were now gone. I was able to save my house by going to HUD and leasing from them, I was so thankful, and remember being so joyful and peaceful with life. I rode my bicycle to school, to continue to get my education, I had my 3 little ones and we seemed very happy and content even with so little. I worked hard, my oldest son even being only 7 or 8 at the time was my best friend, and took on many of the man responsibilities of the house including taking care of me and making sure I was ok. We would ride the bus to my second job, and I would hide all 3 children in the back room, him watching his brother play, and his sister in her car seat as a baby. From there we would go to the mall, I had saved some change from the week, and we went to Dairy Queen, the pet store looking at the dogs, and then all took the bus back home. I had no car, so would go to the grocery store with the kids in the wagon and get groceries, we didn't have much at all, but God always provided and made a way for us, there was always some sort of blessing, money coming from somewhere. I remember one day thinking about how I could get some food, as we had very little, and later that day when I went to check the mail, there was a check in there, just enough to get some basics, potatoes, spam, I made it work. To this day my oldest son remembers those trips as some of his happiest memories, and again, I am very thankful for those experiences. After my daughter is about a year old I will start a new relationship. This being different than the others, he was not physically abusive, however, was somewhat controlling in his own way, and with my co dependency and need to make him happy, we began to have many struggles as we tried to incorporate my controlling behaviors with his parenting of my 3 children. I tried the best I could, but was so protective of my children, and I am sure tried to make up for their every need, to make up for what what we had been through, that he would tell me I was not supportive of him. I was trying very hard to make everyone happy, being in the middle of my children and now what my new relationship wanted and needed. I started going along with things I did not feel were right, I thought I had gained my independence and voice leaving my past relationship, however, some of the same old things crept back in. Often I would start to feel invisible again, not voicing my opinion, or my wants and needs. The more I tried to stand up for myself and the kids, the more I felt our relationship slip, so I settled for many things that I did not approve of, wanting to be the one he needed me to be to support him. I was also going to Graduate School for my Masters degree, I thought I needed to do whatever I could do to make things work as he was graciously allowing me to pursue my dreams and goals. Shortly before I graduated with my Masters degree, I had my 4th child. I graduated from ASU, had my son, and it seemed like we were all very happy, for a while, then it seemed that he wasn't happy. We were struggling to work, pay bills, take care of our family, and I started focusing on him not being happy, as that is what I did, that was my purpose. He told me that he was not happy, but we vowed to keep trying, I remember trying hard to make him realize how much he loved me, however, we eventually separated.

This time raising 4 children. I was working at least 2 jobs, raising my children, and life appeared to be going well. My children by this time were well taken care of, we were not rich by any means, however, all our needs were supplied. I was dating here and there, several fixer uppers as I preferred. I remember one man I was dating smoked pot every day and lived with his Mother, he had nothing to offer me, and to be honest I was not even physically attracted to him, but if I remember correctly he was the first one to respond to me on the dating website so I went with it. We got along ok, played softball together, although he was starting to have grown man tantrums over things. I had paid him to tile my floors and one night as he was staying over, my 17 year old son came home after midnight and he decided that he couldn't come in the house, threw him a quarter for the pay phone, in which I did not agree, I let my son in, they had a physical altercation that night, and I asked him to leave. The most important thing I learned from that relationship at the time was how to tile my floors on my own. I also said I would not get into another relationship like that however, not ever really working on myself or too tired to figure out why I do the things I do, this will continue. Life moved on quickly, my oldest son went into the Marine Corp. My life seemed good, busy, and I continued to have the same type of relationships. I bought my own motorcycle, felt really good, powerful, had my friend at the time help me fix it up, we would go on rides, rallies to Mexico, weekend bike trips, I thought I was having a good time, I was in love again, and going to marry this man, well, that was my plan, once he left his wife. He was very charming, told me all the right things, exactly what I wanted to hear and made me feel good, told me I was fun, and we had many good times together. However, he was married with 2 kids, I used to call him and talk to him only if he was available, meet him secretly at Starbucks and have sex with him in the back of his excursion, wearing the outfit that he requested, then he would go off to work, I wouldn't hear from him but sporadically, and still thought I was in a relationship. After I could no longer live with the guilt I felt for his wife, it had nothing to do with what I was doing to myself, I broke it off with him, even though he continued to text and we would talk, I still thought he was eventually going to leave his wife for me, and figured if I made him go without me and what we shared, that would hurry him up, again, trying to control him, making him make a decision, which never works. I soon after, let him go, probably because I got into another relationship with someone else, not sure. I ran into him at the hospital I worked at a few years later and he told me he was remarried, told me that he left his wife, he also told me that he thought about me, but he met someone else, when I looked at him, he stated and this really hurt me for many years to follow, "that I was not Christian enough for him". As my crazy head spun, and I scurried away from him wondering again, what does he mean? How can I change? How can I be better? How come he did not leave his wife for me? That stung for a long time, I was a Christian, I had a relationship with God and talked to him often on my bike and by myself, how dare he tell me that. The thing that bothers me about that now, is how I let it affect me, those words ring in my ears, my self esteem lower more than it already was, and now realizing, what type of Christian was he? He was doing the same things I was, and he was married. But another message for me to hear and feel that I am not enough. Instead of seeing how hypocritical, and broken he was, I internalized all that to me. From there I continued my life, dating men way below my standards, not feeling that I was worthy of anything better,and staying on this hamster wheel wondering when it stops.

Looking back at my relationships with men in my life I have realized how all of my relationships have been with addicts of some sort. People that I thought I could fix and change to be who I needed and wanted them to be. My self worth was based on how much they loved me and desired me, or how much I thought they loved and desired me. My life changed when I was in a relationship, where my wants and needs were no longer my focus, but their wants and needs became my desire, I completely changed myself to become who I thought they wanted. I learned that I am a caretaker, and put others needs before mine, I learned that I feel sorry for people, regardless of what they do to me, how they treat me, and

I always want to help them, and eventually take over trying to control them and their behaviors. I have realized that this behavior comes from care taking at such a young age, and then through out my life. My relationships with all the men in my life, have had their own issues to tend to, and I constantly tried to tend to them for them. Same as my relationships with my children, when they are struggling with their own addictions, and conflicts in life, I would do anything and everything to take care of them, well take care of them in my way; which means, trying to take their punishments, and their consequences for their behaviors. In one of my previous relationships, I was working on myself, attending counseling, going to groups, doing everything I could to fix things, begging and pleading for him to go to counseling with me or by himself, finding counselors, addiction programs and even was willing to pay for his treatment, all of which he refused. He did attend some groups, however, later I found out he was going to his girlfriend's house instead of meetings, but I remained hopeful that he would eventually change. I continued in this relationship time and time again, and enabled him to continue his behaviors of his addiction.

What I have learned, from continuing to have these types of relationships, is that I was looking to find myself and my self worth in them and in others. My relationships have been abusive, physically, mentally, and severely emotionally. I forgave, tried to forget, and expected that I didn't deserve anything better. Many years of torment, questioning myself, trying to change myself, losing weight because their other girlfriends were small size 2-3. I was not fat at that time but never have I been a size 2-3. Growing my hair, coloring my hair, wearing provocative clothing that I never felt comfortable in to please them. I was going to bars and finding men that were only wanting sex, and having relations with them until they were done with me, and I allowed myself to be treated like this for years. I tolerated so many things in my relationships just to feel loved and wanted. Several years ago I was dating someone who had at least 7 affairs, that I know of. When we first started dating I use to see messages to other women in his phone about how they would leave their nighty's on until he came through, he carried 2 phones one for work of course and one personal. The one for work was the one getting all the text messages and calls. I remember trying to time him getting up in the middle of the night to go to the bathroom so that I could look at his phone, so many messages, from numerous different women. That was only after a few short months of dating. One Valentine's day I was desperately searching though his vehicle and found receipts for at least 3 different gifts of the same thing for all 3 of us. I knew all this was going on, but I loved him, thinking that I could not live without him, as we continued to do this co-dependent dance. My mind would race, thoughts of all the others, thoughts that I was not good enough, trying new different things, trying constantly to please him to make him change. I was trying to control him so much, I could not focus on my own responsibilities. I used to listen to his calls, hiding in my own house where he didn't think I would be, I put GPS trackers in his car to find out where he was going, I followed him or tried to find him on numerous occasions. Once at his apartment I found out an old fling was there to see him, I learned about their relationship as we tried to confront him together, however, he snuck out the back door. Another Valentines Day, he left my house after dinner, I thought something was up, went to his apartment and watched another woman show up at his house around 11 pm. I had made a key one day, he was not aware of, I went inside and there they were getting ready to be intimate in his bed. Another time, I had put my phone on our motorcycle, and GPSd him, followed him to a mall where he was picking up another woman on our motorcycle. I lost my mind, followed them racing down the road, I made him pull over and was not thinking of anything or anybody else, later I realized how bad that situation could have been, I prayed for forgiveness, and vowed to never let that happen again. That worked for a while, I never was that violent or lost my mind like that again, the next time I hid a phone in his truck, and found him at a women's house I had not known, found out they were engaged to be married and she showed me her ring. I briefly talked to her and him, calmly, left, but again forgave and tried to move forward. He promised it would end, that he was sick and would change. This type of behaviors went on for years, so much pain, self doubt, not feeling good enough ever, but always the words, the promises, the hope for change. These behaviors of others were stealing my life, my reality, my happiness.

The last time I allowed anyone to affect me this way was at least 2 years ago. I had set a boundary for myself, knowing that I could not take anymore, I was so involved in all this that I was neglecting my own needs. All the blessings around me that I was not able to see as I could only focus on what was happening in my relationship. I had finally told him if there was anymore cheating at all that I would end our relationship. It was then I realized, I would say things, but that others did not take me seriously, they don't believe you will do anything and won't enforce your boundaries, as you never have before. While he was gone, I got that same old, anxious, nauseous feeling, where I knew something was going on. I tried to call but was neglected as he was "sleeping" This behavior continued, only talking sporadically, and before too long I was getting text messages from his girlfriend I had already caught him with, the one he promised he wouldn't see again. She was texting me how they were together, told me to check her facebook posts, they were together, after our talk, our conversation, my boundaries I had set, he broke them all. It took everything I had to maintain my sanity, I kept going over all this in my mind, all the betrayal, the lies, the sickness, all the turmoil I had put myself through, my boundary, my promise to the girls at group,and to myself. I knew that it was time for me to end this once and for all. I started packing his belongings, before he got to my home, his stuff was in his vehicle, I could no longer do this to myself, repeat this cycle over and over, I made arrangements to take my property back, sell what was considered ours, our motorcycle that he had other women on, and promised myself no matter how hard this was, I was moving forward, no matter how much it hurt, I had to save myself, I had to love myself enough to get out of this and get my life back.

That was the day that I finally got off that hamster wheel, no more doing the same things over and over. That was the day that I took my life back, my power, realized that only I could change my life, only I could make things better with myself, get my happiness and peace back. I knew it was going to be hard, painful, and I felt lonely, confused, devastated to be starting over again, but knew I could get through this, I had to do this if I wanted to see a change in my life. Was it hard? Absolutely, I wanted many times, to go back to what was familiar, fun and safe in the good times, but I stay committed to myself, to getting healthy, I prayed, felt my pain, released it, let go of what I could not control, and my life finally became mine again. Only to realize, that different addictions, the addictions of drugs and alcohol from my past, and now with my family members would be my next battle to face.

As I was working and raising my children, my life took a devastating turn. More addictions came in full force, severe pain, such deep pain that I was very familiar with, but was still so hurtful I didn't think I could move forward. My middle Son started smoking a lot of pot, drinking, hanging out with people that I was very skeptical of, dropped out of high school. My children were always in sports and other activities to keep them grounded, disciplined so that they could make good decisions. Both my oldest sons started playing football with Pop Warner from about age 5 all the way through high school. My second Son was playing football in high school and kept his grades up to play but when it was over he didn't have any ambition or desire for school. He was a Quarterback, a smile that caught every girls attention, and a heart as big as ever. However, he eventually couldn't continue to function with his increasing substance use, so he quit high school, always promised he would get and keep a job, but that soon became just a pattern for him. I watched his life and his potential slowly slip away from him, one bad decision after the next, and the harder I tried to control what was happening and try to fix what was happening, the faster it became out of control, and so dysfunctional in which I had no other options. I couldn't hire any more attorneys, put up bail for him, or change his life for him, he needed to do that, but he couldn't see it, and neither could I yet, as I continued to try to help him no matter the financial, and emotional burden it became for me. He started using Percocet's. I thought I was still trying to keep him from smoking pot every day, as he continued to hide that from me, even though there were signs of him selling and using it, cars pulling up to the house, and him having money even though he wasn't working. Then one day 2 Detectives showed up at my house. My Son just happened to be home and they questioned him about writing prescriptions, I was shocked, this could not be happening. About 6 months after that, and a huge wake up call to me, my Son disclosed that he had been using OxyContin. I then watched this addiction spiral out of control, in between trips to court, him disappearing for long periods of time, and at one time as I thought he was having a panic attack, snorted a bunch of pills up his nose right in front of me. I was lost, broken, confused, and the scariest thing for me was that I did not know what to do, or how to make this better. I thought and was so used to believing that I could always control everything, and make everything work the way it needed to. My son eventually got sentenced to 4 years in prison for writing those prescriptions, he was at this time in a huge addiction. Did I tell you I did and tried everything to try to fix things? I truly would have done anything and everything to help or fix this situation, but it was out of my control. My son in prison, going to Yuma, Douglas, and everywhere else to visit him over the next 4 years. I learned so much about the prison system, how much the system takes advantage of parents and family members that are incarcerated. I was spending tons of money on books for his snacks and hygiene, putting money on the phone for phone calls, and soon before I realized it giving him money to continue to feed his addiction. You see, I thought my son was now getting treatment, in Prison where you can't do drugs anymore, feeling good that he is where he needs to be. Then the frantic phone calls started, "Mom I need 80 dollars right now or they going to kill me". "I owe this for borrowing a soup". I sent too much money to count to him for fear that he was going to get hurt, and he used me that way, as I did not know until much later that he was using Heroin while in prison. My son was released from Prison 4 years later on Parole, going into prison with a Percocet addiction and coming out a Heroin addict, using other's needles, fearful of Hep C. My son had a "friend" pick him up from prison and brought him home. I was happy to see him, eager for him to do what he was supposed to on Parole and keep getting the treatment and help he needed and was supposed to get. This spiraled again, he wasn't clean when he was released, I later found out used on the car ride home, and within 2 months of his Parole time, I had to call his Parole Officer and have him taken back to jail. I had a difficult time with this, but he was now using meth, Heroin, not eating, not taking care of himself, and I truly felt like he was killing himself. He went back to prison to finish his parole time, released and then with the next 4-6 months, was sentenced back to DOC for crimes of drug use, and theft. He learned a trade from his Heroin addicted girlfriend that if he stole things, and then returned them later he would have enough for his addiction. My son was living on the streets, stealing, begging for money from others, and fighting with his girlfriend daily, having physical altercations with her, barely able to function, and I would try to control or fix this on a regular basis. Going to where he was, giving him money for hotel rooms ect. I was trying hard to control my son's addiction, it took me a long time to learn this and to face this, but with lots of work I was soon able to see this and stop enabling him. He is currently back in jail after being released from prison a little over a year ago, his addiction had continued, never hitting rock bottom, trying to use at my home, which I finally set a boundary with, shooting himself accidentally, and never following up with medical treatment or rehab, and before arrested this last time, looked literally like a walking dead person, I am sure would have died, if not arrested. He is now in prison for another 4 and half years, the good news is he is clean and sober, and hopeful. As we talk now, he has clarity, he was rescued, being put in another time out, given an opportunity to change his life, and hopefully share his story with others to help them.

My Daughter my little girl, who worked hard to graduate from high school, and Cosmetology school, and at one point was managing a hair salon barely 20 years old also got involved in drugs. The same familiar pattern, stealing things from home, the hotel rooms, I also tried hard to fix her, paying off title loans, chasing her around all over the city at all times of the night, she eventually went to prison as well and was released in May. Same addiction, same problems, she now faces relapses, last month she attempted suicide, went to a behavioral health hospital for about a week, and then agreed to go to sober living program. She is doing well right now too, a constant fight for her not to go back to what is familiar to her. She recently told me, she does not like living like this, it broke my heart, how much I want this for her, and how much it hurts to not be able to do anything, but support her with her fight to overcome this addiction. I know she will continue to fight, I see myself in her, as she continues to do the same things over and over again. I am hopeful she learns, continues to learn and grow through rehab and recovery programs, so that she can also use her experience to help others. I am aware now through all this, that I can not change her, that I can not fix her, control her behaviors or actions, just as I can not do that for my Son, or anyone in my relationships. I have learned to support, let go and let them and God be in control of their journeys and life paths.

My life changed from having my 4 children home, playing softball, game nights, vacations together, lots of fun and laughter to visiting my son and daughter shackled, chained in and out of county jail, and prison, to being strung out, not able to make decisions, or take care of their own basic needs. Watching them do the same things over and over, and with each day, hoping there is some growth, and long term sobriety, before they die from this disease.

I am sharing my story not to criticize others, their behaviors or pain, but to be open, be honest and vulnerable about my experiences, to hopefully help someone know that we all have life stories to tell, that we should never be afraid of who we are, that we should try to find that strength, our voice, and never let anyone make us think we are less than. Never let others steal our joy, our peace, and happiness. Pray for others to get the help that they need to grow, and let them go when their problems become too unbearable for you to carry. A good friend once told me "you can care but don't carry another's problems". I am very thankful for my experiences, they have made me who I am, made me stronger, and more appreciative of what I have to offer others, without my experiences I could not give others the strength and courage to change themselves and find that peace and happiness we all strive for, that hope and courage to find ourselves, be at peace with who we are, even our mistakes, and our bad decisions. Each day is a new day to be able to learn and grow, and continue to grow everyday.

It took me a very long time to heal from all this, as a matter of fact, I am still healing and will always be in recovery from my enabling and co-dependent behaviors. It took me a very long time not to blame myself for my Children's behaviors. I did not cause them to do what they do, I did not cause this addiction that has such a tight hold on them. I had to learn to love them where they are, support them with limits and boundaries, and most importantly to continue to take care of myself and live my life the best I can. I have learned that I can not control others, my relationships, I have learned that we all have problems, pasts and some sort of addiction to something. I have learned to let others control their own behaviors and finally really and truly realize, that the only person I can control, is myself.

I learned to laugh again, to not blame myself, to love my children, others where they are. My visits and phone calls with my kids in prison and jail are fun times, we laugh, we joke, we hug, we reminisce, we pray together, and we hope for more time to spend together. It is a wonderful relationship, and I know that they are learning, they are going through their journey of life, I realize that I can be a part of their journey, and support them, but that I can not fix or change anything, for them, that is their job, and is up to them, to change, if that is what they choose to do.

It is amazing to me how good God is, he got me through all that tragedy, sadness, and hopelessness. I have an amazing life. My oldest Son is my pride and joy, gave me two precious grandchildren that are blessings of joy and laughter. I have 2 Children in and out of prison, jail, and treatment programs. My youngest son whom I was also worried about due to family history of addiction is on a scholarship at a Christian College.

I am also part of the prison ministry at my church. I go into the jails and teach the women about God and how they can make changes, I wasn't able to reach my daughter before her prison time, but am hoping to reach one of them, and I see much love and hopefulness in them as well.

These life experiences, my past and current relationships with my Children, my friends, my work, and most importantly my relationship with God is what got me to where I am today. I am at peace with who I am, where I am in my life, very content and happy to be me, knowing that I am enough. I realize that I need to take care of myself, and detach from these behaviors that I can not control, or even start to understand. I realized that without me detaching from this disease and these behaviors, that I start to spiral out of control and downward, to where I am not able to help myself or anyone else.

I have realized that I have been inpatient trying to force things into my life, forcing relationships that have not been good for me, tolerating things I should not have tolerated and going against God's plan for my life. I have learned that being patient, surrendering to God what I can not control, letting go of things I can not control, which is everything and anyone but myself ; not letting my life become unmanageable and out of control with other people's problems and addictions, and taking care of myself; are true forms of happiness and joy. I am finally being the woman that I always hoped and dreamed I would be and living according to God's plan. Don't get me wrong, I still wake up every morning wishing and hoping to see my 2 children's healthy faces, to see them have normal, happy lives, and no longer struggling with their addictions. While I am often heartbroken watching them go through this, and am saddened by their continued behaviors; I know that I have done everything I can do for them, and that all I can do now is to continue to pray, support and encourage them to work and maintain their recovery, letting them go to find themselves, and live through their own journey and path.

Life is short, I remind myself every day how grateful, and appreciative of my life, my experiences, and the trials of my past. I continue to grieve for my Son, Daughter, my Mother, and so many others with addictions, and for my past relationships. I trust that there is a plan for my life, that I am living in my purpose, and while I continue to love those that I am not able to save, and control, I realize that by letting them go to live their own life, their own journey and path, that my happiness and my peace of mind are ultimately the most important part of me, and the only thing that I can truly control, and be in charge of.

Printed in the United States
By Bookmasters